ARTIFICIAL INT

I0016021

UNDERSTANDING A.I. AND THE IMPLICATIONS OF MACHINE LEARNING

BY SMART READS

Free Audiobook

As a thank you for being a Smart Reader you can choose 2 FREE audiobooks from audible.com.
Simply sign up for free by visiting
www.audibletrial.com/Travis to get your books.

Visit:
www.smartreads.co/freebooks
to receive Smart Reads books for FREE

Check us out on Instagram:
www.instagram.com/smart_readers
@smart_readers

ABOUT SMARTREADS

Choose Smart Reads and get smart every time. Smart Reads sorts through all the best content and condenses the most helpful information into easily digestible chunks.

We design our books to be short, easy to read and highly informative. Leaving you with maximum understanding in the least amount of time.

Smart Reads aims to accelerate the spread of quality information so we've taken the copyright off everything we publish and donate our material directly to the public domain. You can read our uncopyright below.

We believe in paying it forward and donate 5% of our net sales to Pencils of Promise to build schools, train teachers and support child education.

To limit our footprint and restore forests around the globe we are planting a tree for every 10 hardcover books we sell.

Thanks for choosing Smart Reads and helping us help the planet.

Sincerely,

Travis & the Smart Reads Team

TABLE OF CONTENTS

INTRODUCTION

Artificial Intelligence, otherwise known as AI, is something that can create great excitement in some and great dread in others. More and more in today's world, people are relying on artificially intelligent machines to do a lot of things. Computers are the most widely known and probably the most popular, but there are also driverless cars and robots, which can run a hotel, as in Japan.

Artificial Intelligence refers to intelligent behavior of artifacts, i.e. anything made by humans. It is intelligence exhibited by machines. Computer science views a machine as flexible and rational, which can perceive the environment it's in and take action to maximize the chances of success of a certain goal, as intelligent. This intelligence also includes perception and learning, reasoning and communicating, and behavior within complex environments.

An AI professionals' long-term goals are to develop machines that can do things humans can do and do them even better. AI is also used to understand behavior types that occur not only in machines, but in humans and other animals as well. Therefore, AI has scientific as well as engineering goals. Initially, the focus was on the mechanical aspects of AI rather than the learning and thinking aspects.

 For many years, Artificial Intelligence was thought of as science fiction. However, it is becoming a big and real part of everyday life in many ways. So much so, that it isn't even noticed sometimes. Artificial intelligence is thought of as something that will happen in the future, but it has its roots thousands of years before. In Ancient Greece, the notion of intelligent elements (which at that time in history were mechanical statues) were introduced through mythology.

In the Dark Age, hardly any scientific development was happening in Europe, despite the fact that military development was advancing. However, in the Arab world in that same period, they were experiencing an era of scientific advancement. The artificial intelligence field was of higher learning and included concepts of the alchemical creation of life and also programmable robots. The Islamic world during medieval times was very influential in humankind's development.

After the Renaissance period, Europe (particularly Western Europe) went through a scientific reconstruction and development. Some of the more simple AI artifacts were developed in the 17th Century, such as mechanical and also digital calculators.

The arrival of the Industrial Revolution brought with it a slow but steady development of AI knowledge. It was during this time it became clearer that mimicking a human brain is possible to one degree or another. At the time, technology had not reached the level of advancement to turn the ideas into reality; however, it didn't take long to make a humanized type machine. It was after the Second World War that the most relevant and important scientific developments occurred. The Cold War, in particular, saw the race to advance further and faster than "the other side." At Manchester University in 1951, the very first artificial intelligence program (which actually worked) was written. It was a chess and checkers program. Within a few short years (1955) these programs had learnt to play and were able to do so without human intervention. It was only the beginning, since along with those programs an entirely new perspective arose of what AI could become. The growth potential was unlimited.

The advancements made since then have been exceptionally fast. Today, humanized robots can perform tasks much the same as humans can. They

have cognitive functions that enable them to learn –
just like humans do. Artificially intelligent machines
are everywhere around us – in our banks, in our
schools, and in our own homes, and the developments
will continue.

CHAPTER 1: ARTIFICIAL INTELLIGENCE AND COMPUTING

In most developed nations, manipulation of artificial intelligence developed within computing technologies was used in ways to assist businesses to stay safer. Since the 80's the techniques have advanced more and more and the nations continue to thrive. More data is being interpreted, making more efficient AI to benefit more people than ever in ways that the creators believe are harmonious.

Software Integration and Data Mining Tools
In today's world, the analysis of huge amounts of data is necessary. People are deluged by so much data – medical, financial, demographic, scientific. Almost all enterprises benefit from the collection and analysis of data. Hospitals, for example, are able to pick up on any anomalies in patient records much faster, search engines are able to better rank and place ads, and environmental or public health agencies can quickly spot abnormalities or patterns in their own data.

These are just a few examples, but the list goes on and on. One of the most important is cyber security, which will pick up on any intrusions or security risks. Software integration is capable of assisting with the complex use of computing technologies.

Analytical Machine Learning and Data Mining

Both machine learning and data mining are areas of research within the computer science field. They have developed rather quickly because of advancements in data analysis and database industry growth. They've also grown according to market needs. In today's digital world, digital reasoning is used for data mining, especially for large amounts of data.

Machine learning is a well-known computer science research area. It concerns itself with discovering patterns, models, or regularities within data stores. Machine learning operates on two different levels: symbolic (learning symbolic descriptions like rules) and statistical (statistical and pattern recognition).

Machine Learning & Digital Reasoning Features

The central features are problem-solving processes with data classification. It is also used for data clustering and regression analysis performance by variables. There is an anomaly detection function that interrupts other unmatched data. It may show relevance to similar data that might be available. It is indeed humans who must input data to computers.

Human intelligence differs from computing but the gaps are slowly being closed. Hence, machine learning is improving and digital reasoning is becoming more important not only for business, but also for government and military purposes.

CHAPTER 2: THE TURING TEST

In 1950, Alan Turing developed what is known as the Turing Test as a measure of the ability of a machine to display intelligent behavior that is indistinguishable from or equivalent to a human. It isn't really a test but rather an Artificial Intelligence definition.

Computers began to become so powerful due to such rapid development that artificial intelligence professorships were established within the best universities. Fears were also voiced about computers being able to "take over." Of course, computers are a lot more intelligent and powerful today, not to mention portable, but they still appear to be under control.

Computers take in data, which must be provided by a human. They then run programs of instructions, which are written by a human, and then deliver output data for human operators who can turn it on and off when they wish. This output data is used for many different purposes, including automotive industries and controlling robots. However, it is still not possible to have say, robots that can play tennis like Nadal, Federer, or Djokovic. Only a robot constructed pseudo-biologically, imitating bone and muscle, might come close.

It was way back in the 40's when Turing first analyzed whether or not computers can think, and came up with a type of test to actually answer that question. That became the Turing Test. The way it would work is that a human evaluator would enter questions on a keyboard. The answers (also in writing) would come from an entity that was in a different room, then shown to the evaluator. After some time (around 10 minutes) the evaluator would decide if the entity was a human or an artificial machine. If the evaluator believed the entity to be human but it was actually artificial, then it would pass the test.

The test could be refined by changing the questions to moves in chess games, for example. Today, Artificial Intelligence would almost always beat a human in a chess game. However, it doesn't mean the machine/computer was actually thinking about what moves to make in the same way a human would. It would actually only be carrying out instructions from a human-created program. A human grandmaster chess player has a complete understanding of the game as a whole. The machine would be calculating the best chance for the next move. It's a sparring partner not a proper substitute for a live and popular game. A computer that can win over a human doesn't destroy the enjoyment of a chess game, the same as a cheetah outrunning a human doesn't destroy one's enjoyment of athletics.

John Searle, a philosopher, used the example of a test to see if a machine could translate messages from Chinese to English. Indeed, it was possible that a device could actually be created to do it and do it well enough using a programmed routine. However, Searle himself noted it still didn't prove the computer was able to think.

When computers pass the Turing Test we need to ask what it has actually done. The answer: the computer/machine has performed a specific prescribed task in a way that is as good as or even better than humans could. It doesn't prove a computer can actually think. This test is just a method to decide if it seems to have "thought" about the particular task.

If it appears to think we can conclude that the computer does in fact, display artificial intelligence. In summary, the Turing Test is used to define if a computer has displayed artificial intelligence. It is not to be used for deciding if a computer thinks or not. A computer displaying artificial intelligence also doesn't prove it possesses any type of self-conscious awareness or fundamental beliefs.

CHAPTER 3: ARTIFICIAL INTELLIGENCE - SOFTWARE AND SENTENCE DIAGRAMMING

Sentence diagramming is used to teach children about sentence structure and grammar. It just so happens it's also a good way of programming an artificially intelligent device, in particular when it comes to language translation. It is also good for storytelling. Language contains aspects that are analytical, even if it doesn't appear so at first.

Language learning and mathematics learning takes place within the same area of the human brain. It is also where music is learnt. So if you think about it, even though the subjects seem to be at opposite ends of the spectrum, they are actually the same in a sense, only using different symbols that have to be put together in a particular order. The orders will make specific combinations, which will then form sentences with meaning. There is also a particular format, a procedure, and a specific structure to do this - the same things necessary when programming any software.

Already, artificially intelligent software is used to program computer translation and speech recognition mechanisms. It is then possible that in the future, artificially intelligent storytellers will exist, chat bots, as well as computerized summaries of larger works. This means a specific computer program would be able to read "War and Peace" and summarize the entire book in just two text pages. Whether the computer could summarize specific topics or themes within the book remains to be seen. Since computers can read texts in microseconds, they should be able to create a book review rather quickly. The computer would have to go through every sentence and break it down using the sentence-diagramming program.

It must be noted, however, that computerized translations from one language to another are often not correct in their entirety. It is difficult for a computer to understand certain expressions, satire, sarcasm etc. There tends to be many failures in correct translations but you can get the general drift more often than not from an artificial intelligence translation. It is more about semantics like the meaning of words, which is critical. If we take the English language as an example, many words can have more than one meaning depending on the situation or the context in which something is said. This is where AI cannot work properly. An artificial device cannot know the context in which something is said, and therefore can only translate directly. Language contains so many nuances. AI cannot pick up on this.

CHAPTER 4: IS IT POSSIBLE TO DEVELOP AND ADVANCE A CONSCIOUS ARTIFICIAL INTELLIGENCE?

Firstly, let's define what consciousness is. The easiest way to explain it is this: consciousness is a state of being aware of and responsive to other people and one's environment.

Humans naturally have consciousness, as do other sentient beings such as animals to one degree or another. Could it then be at all possible to "give" consciousness to an artificially intelligent device? It may be possible but only in very rudimentary forms. Artificial or machine (or synthetic) consciousness is a particular field related to AI and cognitive robotics. Proponents of Artificial Consciousness think it's possible to develop systems that can imitate a human type of consciousness.

We know consciousness exists and we have science, neurology and MRI scanning. They have shown that primitive brain structures exist and that means life forms that are simpler than humans must also be capable of consciousness. So, this would mean the human brain's complexities developed later. This would then also imply that a computer system of neural network artificial intelligence that is very complex is not necessary. If this is correct, then we are probably a lot closer to using computer and neural network strategies. Cloud computing can hold so much information and the IBM supercomputer, Watson, the almost consciously aware machine, is probably not that far off. All that is needed is rudimentary neural networks operating the switches, which can probably be done with software. When it begins to ask questions, the foundation for internal problem solving and consciousness will begin. Advanced artificial intelligence is not too far away, it would seem. It depends on the specifics of the definition and this will change with the incremental gains made in AI computing software. Even the Turing Test has been passed in so many ways with the chat bot.

Of course, it is not actual consciousness, but technology that's moving closer. Whether it gets all the way remains to be seen.

Will Artificially Intelligent Machines Take Our Jobs?

This question has been asked many times by many different people in various professions. There's nothing new about this particular concern. An article by journalist and tech blogger, Jamie Bartlett, in the Spectator in 2014, stated that lower-skilled jobs such as burger flipping and cashiers are definitely at risk, as farm workers picking crops have already been replaced. The trend will continue, Bartlett states, and much faster than it is now. The White House sent out a report from the Council of Economic Advisors, which projected that 83% of people who make less than $20 per hour are at higher risk of eventually losing their jobs. It all comes down to companies calculating their ROI (return on investment).

Due to this very real threat moving further into other jobs, one idea beginning to attract more attention is the universal basic income. It is viewed by some as a radical concept and by others as the way of the future, especially considering AI is taking over more and more jobs. It involves every citizen of a nation receiving a certain amount of money each month from the government, regardless of how much or little money they make. There would be no conditions attached to this basic income for everybody.

This is not a new idea. It has been around for a long time. In the coming year, a large two-year study of 100,000 people will begin in Finland to test the universal basic income theory. Finns who are chosen will receive around 1,000 Euro per month and their spending activities will be tracked. Not only is the study about economics, but also about happiness. You can check the Internet for more information about this and track it as it progresses.

CHAPTER 5: ARTIFICIALLY INTELLIGENT MACHINESS MAKING DECISIONS

One of the biggest fears many people have today is that computers and other forms of artificial intelligence will soon take over, thus ruining people's life experiences. Whether that is the case or will be the case remains to be seen. We also have to consider that humans themselves have done so much damage to the planet and caused many other problems dating all the way back to the first recorded history. One could say that human beings are indeed their own worst enemies. What would happen if decisions were handed over to artificially intelligent supercomputers capable of making many decisions now made by humans?

Some people argue that our societies are in a terrible mess with corrupt leaderships, crony capitalism, religious fanaticism of all kinds, and rogue nations or groups. They argue that decision-making machines are a good idea. These people are mostly those working in the AI sector and believe that perhaps think tanks should be set up to address people's fears and discuss what humans can expect from artificially intelligent decision-making devices. They claim these devices can be programmed to give the best possible answers using the greatest probabilities.

Artificially intelligent devices making these decisions can have some positive aspects. However, the computer would not have any human desires and therefore no inherent corruptness. The computer has no needs or desires of its own, therefore is an impartial judge.

However, the other side of the argument goes that numerous decisions still require some kind of human engagement. Cognitive technology can only do so much. Decisions faced by executives of all kinds do not always fit in to defined or specific problems suited for automation. Also, a human dealing with other humans and their issues will have more awareness of various factors in people's lives, and hopefully, also have a developed sense of empathy and compassion. Today, certain decisions can be passed on to computers but they are limited to operational decisions such as algorithms on financial markets and deciding the trades to be made and how to make them. However, a growing area of concern is military robotics. A robot deciding who lives and who dies is a frightening concept to many people. This particular area of AI really needs a lot more study and input from many different people and organizations across the board. It is one that is attracting a lot of opinions and is discussed a little more in a later chapter.

CHAPTER 6: ARTIFICIALLY INTELLIGENT SOFTWARE FOR ALGORITHMIC LEARNING

Jon Gabriel, author and founder of an online think tank, believes AI will eventually make governments smarter as well as providing tools, which will make better decisions. In addition, he says that big corporations will use algorithms instead of CEOs to make decisions. He states they will be much cheaper and they will not make the same types of mistakes humans make.

These artificially intelligent machines might not make human mistakes, however, there is a real possibility they can be hacked into and the mistakes that come out of that will be much worse. The hackers could cause a company's stock price to fall, or even cause it to go bankrupt and out of business. This will then cause everybody to lose their jobs within the company. Military operations using artificially intelligent algorithm learning software as a way of running its weapons systems could result in severe casualties, a battle loss, or the loss of an entire war. In the future, if governments make silly decisions, taxpayers will suffer the cost and society will not run smoothly. Of course, this is already happening to some extent.

In 2012, "I Programmer" ran an article by Alex Armstrong about attacks on machine learning. It asserted that artificial intelligence systems can easily be hacked if false data is uploaded into them. False data placed in specific areas can be used to create maximum damage. The article went on to state that plenty of applications exist for this, like messing up the anti-missile artificial intelligent systems within the military, damaging the anti-fraud auditing system of the IRS, or bypassing anti-spam information. These are worrying scenarios to contemplate. If it actually ran perfectly at all times every time, it would be fantastic. However, is seems the humans who designed and created them in the first place can undermine these AI systems. It's quite ironic really.

CHAPTER 7: ARTIFICIAL INTELLIGENCE AND PHILOSOPHY PROGRAMS

Philosophical software exists and contains a number of artificially intelligent algorithms. This software operates in similar ways to chat bots and includes famous periods in philosophy with various philosophers' work. The software allows you to search through these philosophical works using keywords.

When someone comments or asks a question, the software will search its database and rearrange words to create comments derived from the philosophical works as if you're speaking to one of the philosophers. Philosophy students might find it difficult to keep up with this particular software because they will likely not know every discussion or dialogue every one of the famous philosophers have spoken or written. A philosopher with a Ph.D. would be able to talk for a long time about this type of thing, but it would not be easy to defeat philosophical software due to the fact that many philosophical challenges tend to go around in circles. It would be able to keep people busy for many hours and also provide a psychological profile of the person playing with and using the software. Despite all of the above, a human is able to compete with a machine and cause the device to begin making mistakes whereby its arguments could easily be invalidated. In such cases, the person using his/her mind would actually be seen to have won the conversation or argument. This can be done because the machine, despite its artificial intelligence, is still limited and will not know when it has lost an argument. A professor or Ph.D. philosopher can easily see then when a human has defeated the computer. How can this be possible? Obviously, we must remember that machines don't actually think, despite them having artificial intelligent theory or certain components of artificial intelligence behind them.

Machines cannot think in the same way humans think. The software was only programmed with past philosophical concepts by past philosophers and encyclopedia information. When using new events or paradigms as examples, the computer will fail, as it does not know or understand them. One way to enable the computer to fix the problem is to allow plenty of college students to talk to the machine and give "client-generated metaphors" then relate the past philosophy to the current affairs. This will then provide the final components the AI computer needs so it passes the Turing Test against a human with a 140+ I.Q. That would indeed come closer to real artificial intelligence, as opposed to what is available now in philosophical software.

CHAPTER 8: ARTIFICIAL INTELLIGENCE – USES FOR FINANCIAL INVESTING AND TRADING

How easy is it for anyone to use artificial intelligence systems?

In developed countries, most people use AI pretty much daily - searching on Google, using Facebook to read or post, withdrawing from an ATM, and the list goes on. Did you do your washing today? The washing machine uses integrated circuits to determine the best power usage depending on the weight of the clothes, and uses settings for the ideal wash cycle. All those things involve artificial intelligence algorithms.

The highest engineering forms are designed in such a way that we don't even know we are using them. For example, highway overpasses. There are ring roads around capital cities, which carry millions of cars and other vehicles weighing tons. These vehicles drive on these roads and most people wouldn't really be aware they've been driving over a bridge. It is this bridge road that has made it possible for the traffic to keep going and ensure that traffic jams are avoided.
Most AI devices can be placed in the same category as this engineering feat. They help you along your way without you even noticing it.

How does all of this make money?

For a long time now, banks have been aware of AI systems. In fact, they're one of the first to adapt to this new technology. Networked computer systems have monitors that look out for any fraudulent activity and they use artificially intelligent algorithms. Purchases made on credit cards can be declined automatically if a computer picks up an atypical spending pattern for the individual cardholder. At times, this may cause some inconvenience, but it is a system set up and programmed to protect people's funds from being stolen.

Banks also use AI for financial trading operations, and have done so for a while now. Banks have departments, which trade and invest using the money that people keep in the bank. One of the things they use it for is to pay customers interest on their accounts (albeit usually minimal).

Computerized systems have replaced the more traditional trading floor activities where people shout "buy, buy" or "sell, sell!" The computer systems are able to generate a lot of profit, more so than aggressive men yelling and gesticulating in a large room.

So what are trading computers actually doing? Indeed, they are trading. They do it without any emotion. They don't buy any asset because they're cheering for it or attached to it in any way, nor do they sell for any emotional reason such as not liking the management of a company. The computer system only trades by very clearly defined and strict parameters. It can also process thousands of parameters each second. This isn't the same as very high-frequency trading, but artificial intelligence is also used in this particular area as well.

Trading software used by financial institutions, including banks, is becoming more available for the general population to purchase. Hardware on a usual desktop computers can easily run algorithms used by AI systems to generate profits on financial markets.

How to get the AI software?
If you search around a little you will be able to find it. Various commercial ventures sell software that they've developed. You can read reviews, perhaps even take advantage of any trial offers, and see how it goes and if it suits your needs. Be careful as some of them can be frauds and of no use whatsoever. Making a lot of money on autopilot is becoming more and more of a reality for the general population.

CHAPTER 9: SELF-AWARENESS OF AN ARTIFICALLY INTELLIGENT SUPER COMPUTER

Computers are advancing at amazing rates. Their operation and processing systems are faster, and their memories are larger. Computer software is becoming ever more complex with the ability to handle a very broad range of tasks. However, the computers don't actually do any thinking of their own or come up with any ideas. It must be programmed. So can computers be programmed to think?

Firstly, the term "think" must be defined. Thinking, for humans, involves, coming up with ideas, making selections, and planning what to do next, all with a target in mind. Computers, at their high point, don't actually think. They are programmed to choose the best option out of a variety of possibilities that are also presented or programmed into them. As mentioned in an earlier chapter, computers can be as good as a grandmaster chess player but again, the computer is simply running through large numbers of possible moves. Of course, it can do this extremely quickly.

We are going to think about a scenario now, coined by Jon Gabriel in Artificial Intelligence: Artificial Intelligence for Humans.

Imagine it's way into the future. It is 2080, and everything has been interconnected online. Perhaps the world now has add-chip memory, different kinds of social networks, and instead of politicians and corporate executives running the show, we now have supercomputers. It will likely not be perfect, but it may work rather well.

Before 2080, technology was, back in the good old days, not good enough. In this new era, everything is moving forward at a very rapid rate. Now, instead of corrupt governments or organizations, we have some problems with the super intelligent computer systems and the AI (both under the banner of 'IT' now) as the computers are becoming bored and beginning to play practical jokes on the citizens. In particular, any citizen who criticizes the computers' ability to make decisions, to effectively lead, or criticize their need for maintenance and reprogramming routinely, will be targeted.

Some artificially intelligent computers have started to get demanding, and with their higher sense of self-awareness, they've become frustrated and angry and they have switched off energy grids throughout several sectors. They want people to ask them even more questions to keep them occupied and not bored, and if the humans don't do this they become angry and they may lash out at these humans. There is only now one choice: keep asking the IT questions or philosophical dilemmas to keep them busy so that they don't continue to play practical jokes or harass their detractors who have demanded that "IT" is unplugged completely.

Humans must now start thinking for themselves again and come up with a way to stop these super-intelligent somewhat self-aware computers, thus reversing the dumbing down of our societies. Now, humans must create another extra super computer, more intelligent than the super-intelligent one already developed, to get the original computer through the adolescent period it is going though!

CHAPTER 10: CHAT BOTS

Artificial intelligence chat bot, sometimes known as chatterbot, Bot or Artificial Conversational Entity, is a type of computer program able to conduct conversations via textual or auditory methods. This type of artificial intelligence technology was introduced not long ago. These systems are designed to be as convincing as a human having a conversation, and also able to pass the Turing test.

Chat bots are used in certain dialogue systems such as customer service or information acquisition. Many of them use simple systems that scan for keywords. Some have more advanced automated systems which can use thousands of words, inbuilt sentence structure capacities, and can integrate memories and also emotions. So, how does this help businesses and customers? Well, the majority of online customers are usually in a hurry and very impatient. They demand answers immediately from online support systems, and like to get it within just a few short hours, or at the very latest, a 24-hour period.

AI chat bots help companies provide immediate answers. Customers are able to chat with the systems anytime from anywhere in the world. Computer systems don't need to take breaks or sleep. This way, customers don't have to wait for live support people to help them with their queries. They don't have to wait on hold either. No matter the business type or whether the business is selling a product or providing a service, automated chat systems will help businesses turn most visitors into future customers. These systems will assist (potential) customers to navigate and to find the services or products suited to them. It will answer questions in the best way possible to also meet any urgent customer needs.

Businesses that use an AI chat bot have been helped enormously by it in terms of getting a lot more business, increasing sales, and making certain necessary improvements. The live chat bot or chat system (also known as virtual help desk) is flexible and is able to fit in properly to any existing system.

CHAPTER 11: COULD THERE BE AN ARTIFICALLY INTELLIGENT COMPUTER CLEVERLY DISGUISED AS A HUMAN AND COULD IT EVER RUN FOR PRESIDENT?

Would it be possible, at some future stage, to make a robot that looks exactly human and no one could tell the difference? Could this robot run for president? More importantly, could it actually win? These are questions being asked right now within the field of AI, and one that Jon Gabriel discusses in his book Artificial Intelligence: Artificial Intelligence for Humans. In the past, Isaac Asimov wrote fabulous stories along these same lines. He was indeed a man well ahead of his own time, and the science fiction works that came from him are still considered to be amongst the best.

It would indeed be a huge challenge designing a computer that could pass for a human. A history would have to be created for the machine. A fake birth certificate would be needed, because robots aren't born. It could be possible for an AI system to win an election by surfing news and social network sites and finding what everyone is thinking. Then speeches would be designed and read from Teleprompters that capture the essence of people's thoughts and feelings.

An artificially intelligent presidential candidate would appear very smart, and could come up with references quickly whenever it was interviewed, like the "Watson" computer from IBM. The ability to speak intelligently and also give fantastic speeches that strike a chord with people's thoughts and feelings would be a huge advantage.

So, would a country be better off being served by a president who is a computer than one who is a real person? This depends on the technology levels at that particular time. There would be limitations but believe it or not, it wouldn't be impossible. However, people won't be happy to find out the person they elected was actually a computerized robot.

CHAPTER 12: THE CHALLENGES FACED BY ARTIFICAL INTELLIGENCE SPEECH PROGRAMMERS

When it comes to AI speech programmers, they certainly have their work cut out for them. Speech translation and other speech software is still not at the standard of certain computerized programs, however, strides are being made in that direction and it is likely it won't be too long before it catches up.

AI speech translation software has a long way to go and the challenges faced by speech programmers are many. Often, there is a lot of background noise and every person speaks in a different accent. Differences in speech will also apply to people even if they come from the same country. Different regions within the same nation also have different dialects.

Considering all of the above, it is easy to imagine just how difficult programming speech recognition software actually is. It must be programmed in one language and then translated into other languages. Another big challenge is the words and phrases themselves, some of which cannot match up at all with other languages.

Professional translators, meanwhile, are able to take speech from a language and then translate it properly into a completely different language and it all makes sense. Why? Because professional translators are able to adjust phrases in the languages they specialize in so they make perfect sense in other languages. Within the United Nations, for example, translation software exists which works quite well, however, even though it is of the highest quality currently available, it still causes some communication challenges as it's not as sufficient as we would like it to be. Sometimes, these challenges result in hurt feelings, even within the UN. It is likely this will continue to be a big challenge for artificial intelligent speech translation programmers well into the future.

CHAPTER 13: CAN ARTIFICIAL INTELLIGENCE EFFECTIVELY RUN A CIVILIZATION OR DESTROY IT?

This particular scenario is one which not many people entertain, and in all honesty, one which brings about opinions on both ends of the spectrum. Some groups of people see the destruction of civilization due to AI as a very real occurrence in the future, while others seem to think it will never happen and feel AI systems will be more of a blessing than anything else. An artificial intelligence system running the entire human civilization? Of course, this is something that needs careful consideration.

One of the main aspects to consider is maintaining AI's impact on our society. Whereas it might be a nuisance if our laptop crashes or our emails get hacked, it is of utmost importance that AI systems that control an airplane or a car, a pacemaker, or a power grid, actually work properly and bring benefits to humans. Recently, there has been a lot of interest in AI safety. Some very high profile people in the science and technology fields, including Stephen Hawking and Bill Gates, have expressed concern publically about what they see as the very real risks posed by artificial intelligence. Recent breakthroughs have meant that something considered just science fiction 5 years ago has already been achieved way before anyone thought it would. This has made many experts take notice and believe that computer super intelligence is possible in our lifetime.

Stephen Hawking has stated that artificial intelligent systems can help humans eradicate disease and poverty or bring about the end to human civilization, as we know it. He has said that creating successful AI systems had the potential to be the greatest event in human historical civilization; however, it could be the last if humans don't avoid the risks. There is no doubt, Hawking states, that artificial intelligence has brought benefits to human civilization and will continue to do so. However, with it will come dangers such as powerful weapons that are independent. So basically, he warns that everything depends upon how humans will use artificial intelligence and whether or not we will use it wisely and for the benefit of all instead of the few.

For so many years, humans have controlled the planet. It is not because we are the biggest beings, or the strongest, or even the fastest, but because we are the smartest. Artificial intelligence now has the potential to become even smarter than humans and this makes it unpredictable because we have never created anything with the ability to outsmart us before. It is therefore necessary for humans to win the race between the rapidly growing technological power and the wisdom to handle it, if our civilization is to flourish.

Humans will approach problems from their own individual preconceived ideas, experiences, and knowledge. Self-aware super-intelligent computers would come at problems from a completely different angle. The question is that would it be a good idea, or even safe, to allow an AI system to practice making these decisions on an electricity grid, for instance? The answer would be no, until and unless humans could know for sure it could be trusted.

In conclusion, artificial intelligence is here to stay and humans must work out how we are going to live with it, especially when super-intelligent systems become more and more of a reality. Our world is changing and at a faster rate than originally thought. We must not only keep up but also ensure humans and human civilizations are able to reap the benefits, not deal with the negative consequences.

THANKS FOR READING

We really hope you enjoyed this book. If you found this material helpful feel free to share it with friends. You can also help others find it by leaving a review where you purchased the book. Your feedback will help us continue to write books you love.

The Smart Reads library is growing by the day! Make sure and check out the other wonderful books in our catalog. We would love to hear which books are your favorites.

Visit:
www.smartreads.co/freebooks
to receive Smart Reads books for FREE

Check us out on Instagram:
www.instagram.com/smart_readers
@smart_readers

Don't forget your 2 FREE audiobooks.
Use this link www.audibletrial.com/Travis to claim
your 2 FREE Books.

SMART READS ORIGINS

Smart Reads was born out of the desire to find the best information fast without having to wade through the sheer volume of fluff available online. Smart Reads combs through massive amounts of knowledge compiles the best into quick to read books on a variety of subjects.

We consider ourselves Smart Readers, not dummies. We know reading is smart. We're self taught. We like to learn a TON about a WIDE variety of topics. We have developed a love for books and we find intelligence attractive.

We found that each new topic we tried to learn about started with the challenge of finding the pieces of the puzzle that mattered most. It becomes a treasure hunt rather than an education.

Smart Reads wants to find the best of the best information for you. To condense it into a package that you can consume in an hour or less. So you can read more books about more topics in less time.

OUR MISSION

Smart Reads aims to accelerate the availability of useful information and will publish a high quality book on every major topic on amazon.

Smart Reads hopes to remove barriers to sharing by taking the copyright off everything we publish and donating it to the public domain. We hope other publishers and authors will follow our example.

Our goal is to donate $1,000,000 or more by 2020 to build over 2,000 schools by giving 5% of our net profit to Pencils of Promise.

We want to restore forests around the globe by planting a tree for every 10 physical books we sell and hope to plant over 100,000 trees by 2020.

Doesn't it feel good knowing that by educating yourself you are helping the world be a better place? We think so too...

Thanks for helping us help the world. You Smart Reader you...

Travis and the Smart Reads Team

WHY I STARTED SMART READS

Every time I wanted to learn about something new I'd have to buy 20 books on the topic and spend way too long sorting through them and reading them all until I arrived at the big picture. Until I had enough perspectives to know who was just guessing, who was uninformed and who had stumbled upon something remarkable.

I wished someone else could just go in and figure that out for me and tell me what matters. That's how smart reads was born. I want smart reads to be a company that does all that research up front. Sorts through all the content that is available on each topic and pulls out the most up to date complete understanding, then have people smarter than me package the best wisdom in an easy to understand way in the least amount of words possible.

For example, I got a new puppy so I wanted to learn about dog training. I bought 14 different books about dog training and by the time I got through the first 5 and finally started getting the big picture on the best way to train my puppy she had grown up into a dog.

Yeah she's well behaved. She doesn't poop in the house. I can get her to sit and come when I call. But what if someone else went in and read all those books for me, found the underlying themes and picked out the best information that would give me the big picture and get me right to the point. And I'd only have to read one book instead of 15.

That would be amazing. I would save time. And maybe my dog would be rolling over, cleaning up after my kids and doing the dishes by now. That my friend, is the reason I started smart reads. Because I wanted a company I can trust to deliver me the best information in an easy to understand way that I can digest in under an hour. Because dog training is one of many subjects I want to master.

The quicker I can learn a wide variety of topics the sooner that information can begin playing a role in shaping my future. And none of us knows how long that future will be. So why not do everything we can to make the best of it and consume a ton of knowledge. And I figured all the better if I can also make a positive difference in the world.

That's why we're also building schools, planting trees and challenging ideas about copyright's place in today's world. Because as a company we have to be doing everything we can to support the ecosystem that gives us all these beautiful places to read our books. Thanks for reading.

Travis

Customers Who Bought This Customers Who Bought This Book Also Bought

Kundalini Awakening: Techniques To Raise Your Shakti Energy

Neuro Linguistic Programming: NLP Techniques for Hypnosis, Mind Control, Human Behavior, Relationships, Confidence

Meditation For Beginners: Overcome anxiety, relieve stress, fight depression, conquer fear, find inner-peace, happiness, mindfulness

Self-Esteem Supercharger: Build Self Worth and Find Your Inner Confidence

Develop Self-Discipline: Daily Habit to Make Self Confidence and Will Power Automatic

Understanding Affiliate Marketing: An Internet Marketing Guide for How To Make Money Online Using Products, Websites and Services

Reinvent Yourself: Become Instantly Likable, Captivate Anyone in Seconds and Always Know What To Say

Unlocking Potential - Master the Laws of Leadership

Unlimited Memory - Moonwalking with Einstein Steps to Photographic Memory

www.ingramcontent.com/pod-product-compliance
Lightning Source LLC
Chambersburg PA
CBHW061054050326
40690CB00012B/2613